Science Vocabulary

Insect Homes

Lydia Carlin

SCHOLASTIC INC.

NEW YORK • TORONTO • LONDON • AUCKLAND • SYDNEY
MEXICO CITY • NEW DELHI • HONG KONG • BUENOS AIRES

ISBN-13: 978-0-545-00739-9 / ISBN-10: 0-545-00739-9

Photos Credits:

Cover: © David Kjaer/Nature Picture Library; title page: © Mitsuaki Iwago/Minden; contents page, from top: © Noel Hendrickson/Digital Vision (RF)/Getty Images, © Jena Cumbo/The Image Bank/Getty Images, © Ingo Arndt/Nature Picture Library, © Christian Ziegler/Minden Pictures; page 4: © Noel Hendrickson/Digital Vision (RF)/Getty Images; page 5: © David Kjaer/Nature Picture Library; page 7, top left: © Mark Chappell/Animals Animals; page 7, top right: © Leroy Simon/Visuals Unlimited/Getty Images; page 7, bottom left: © Philippe Clement/Nature Picture Library; page 7, bottom right: © John and Lisa Merrill/Riser/Getty Images; page 8: © Jena Cumbo/The Image Bank/Getty Images; page 9, top left: © Tim Ridley/Dorling Kindersley/Getty Images; page 9, top right: © Kim Taylor/BCIUSA; page 9, bottom left: © Kim Taylor/npl/Minden; page 9, bottom right: © Dorling Kindersley/Getty Images; page 9, middle: © Dorling Kindersley/Getty Images; page 10: © Mitsuhiko Imamori/ Minden Pictures; page 11: © Joel Sartore/National Geographic (RF)/Getty Images; page 11, inset: © David Scharf/Science Faction/Getty Images; page 12: © Suzi Eszterhas/Nature Picture Library; page 13: © Phone Labat J.M./Rouqu/Peter Arnold, Inc.; page 14: © Gerry Ellis/Minden Pictures; page 15, top left: © Gerry Ellis/Minden Pictures; page 15, top right: © Michael and Patricia Fogden/Minden Pictures; page 15, bottom left: © Ingo Arndt/Minden Pictures; page 15, bottom right: © Ingo Arndt/Nature Picture Library; page 16: © Mitsuhiko Imamori/Minden Pictures; page 17, top left: © Premaphotos/Nature Picture Library; page 17, top right: © Philippe Clement/Nature Picture Library; page 17, bottom left: © Kim Taylor/Nature Picture Library; page 17, bottom right: © Kim Taylor/Nature Picture Library; page 18: © Piotr Naskrecki/Minden Pictures; page 19: © Gerry Ellis/Minden Pictures; page 20: © Christian Ziegler/Minden Pictures; page 21: © Credit: Milkins/OSF/Animals Animals; page 22: © Piotr Naskrecki/Minden Pictures; page 23: © Philippe Clement/Nature Picture Library; page 24: © Konrad Wothe/Minden Pictures; backcover: © John William Banager/Getty Images.

Photo research by Dwayne Howard
Design by Holly Grundon

12 11 10 9 8 7 6 5 4 3 2   8 9 10 11 12 13/0

Printed in the U.S.A.
First printing, March 2008

Contents

Chapter 1

Insects Have Homes!

People live in homes.

wasp nest

Insects live in homes, too!

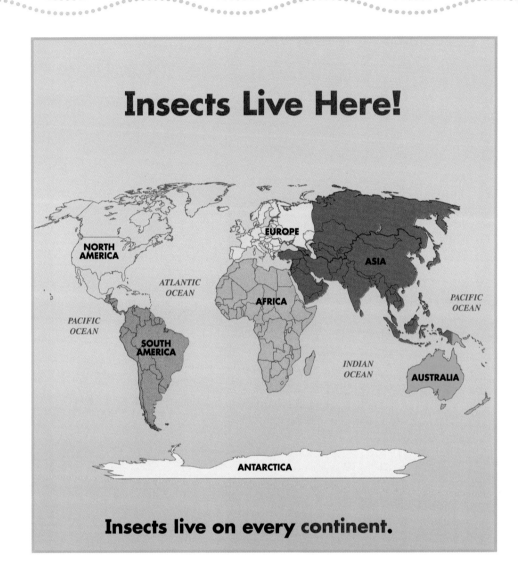

Insects Live Here!

NORTH AMERICA

EUROPE

ASIA

ATLANTIC OCEAN

AFRICA

PACIFIC OCEAN

PACIFIC OCEAN

SOUTH AMERICA

INDIAN OCEAN

AUSTRALIA

ANTARCTICA

Insects live on every continent.

Insects live everywhere on Earth. They live in warm places like Africa. Some even live in cold places like Antarctica.

honeybee

butterfly

cricket

praying mantis

Insects live in **hives** and holes. They also live on plants. Let's learn all about their homes!

Chapter 2

Homes Down Low

Many insects make their homes on the ground.
Turn over a rock. What is underneath?

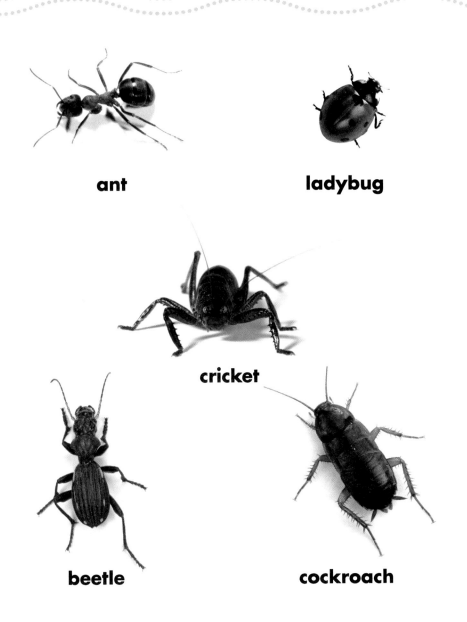

ant

ladybug

cricket

beetle

cockroach

You might see some of these bugs! Rocks help them stay cool and safe from predators.

This grasshopper blends in with the grass.

What else lives on the ground? Grasshoppers! Their green color helps them hide in the tall grass of **meadows**.

Close Up!

An aphid looks like this close up.

aphids

Tiny aphids live on plants. The plants are their home. The plants are also their dinner. Munch, munch!

anthill

AFRICA

This anthill is in Africa.

Take a look at this huge anthill. Wow! It is big enough for cheetahs to rest on it.

Fast Fact

A million termites can live in one mound.

termite mound

This is a termite **mound**. Termites build them by mixing dirt with their sticky spit. Some mounds are taller than houses!

Chapter 3

Homes Up High

Some insects like the high life! Trees all over the world are filled with lots and lots of busy bugs.

leaf-mimic katydid

bullseye silkmoth

treehopper

flannel moth

All of these insects live in one tree in the rain forest. In fact, scientists have found more than 2,000 kinds of bugs sharing a single tree!

A wasp builds a paper nest.

Wasps build nests in trees. They chew up little bits of wood to make a soft, wet **pulp**. Then they use their legs to shape the pulp.

When the pulp dries, it becomes a paper nest.
Can you believe it? Wasps used teamwork to
make all of these nests!

Fast Fact

Weaver ants are also called "tailor ants."

This is silk.

Weaver ants build nests in trees, too. Like spiders, they are able to make a special kind of thread called **silk**.

weaver-ant nest

They use the silk to weave together leaves.
It takes hundreds of hard-working weaver ants
to make one nest. Incredible!

Chapter 4

More Amazing Homes

army-ant cluster

Army ants build a new home each night.
How? They grab onto one another and form
a **cluster**. Sticking together keeps them safe!

diving beetle

Fast Fact

This insect's back legs are shaped like paddles.

Diving beetles live in ponds and lakes. They are great swimmers and can hold their breath underwater for a long time.

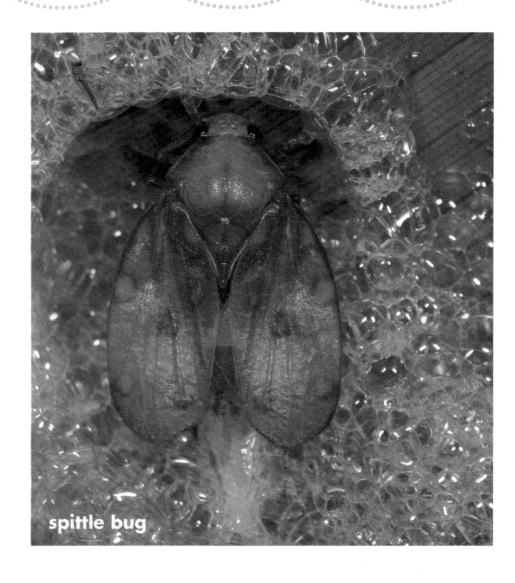

spittle bug

Where do spittle bugs live? In blobs of their own spit! Spit may seem icky to you. But to them, it is home sweet home.

Glossary

cluster (**kluhss**-tur): a group that stands close together

continent (**kon**-tuh-nuhnt): one of seven large land masses on earth: Asia, Africa, Europe, North America, South America, Australia, and Antarctica

hive (**hive**): a home where bees live

meadow (**med**-oh): a field of grass

mound (**mound**): a tall, rounded hill

paddle (**pad**-uhl): a short, wide oar used to move boats

pulp (**puhlp**): a soft wet mass of little wood pieces that dries into paper

silk (**silk**): thin, soft threads that can be woven together